fotografs of bones

three seasons of poetry

adam perry

MONKEY PUZZLE PRESS
BOULDER, COLORADO

The following poems from this book have previously been published: "Sudden Death // Simple Man" and "Worship, Salvation and Prayer" appeared in *Flaneur Foundry* (Columbia Unversity, New York, NY); "The Precipice Went Slack" appeared in *Zero Ducats* (Missoula, MT); "Ballad" appeared in *Whrrds* (Naropa University, Boulder, CO); "An Allegheny of Divine Wisdom" appeared in *Tendrel Magazine* (Naropa University, Boulder, CO); "Dear Horizon" appeared in *Arthur Magazine* (Los Angeles, CA); "Bad Thoughts Escape Through Holes in the Page" appeared in *Monkey Puzzle* (Boulder, CO).

Cover Photo by Kate Joyce
www.kate-joyce.com
Sculptures in photo by Magdalena Abakanowicz
in Grant Park, Chicago, IL

Cover & Book Design by Nate Jordon and Irene Joyce

ISBN 978-0-9801650-2-9

Monkey Puzzle Press
3116 47th St.
Boulder, CO   80301
www.monkeypuzzleonline.com

Publisher's Note

I founded Monkey Puzzle Press in 2007 during my graduate studies at the Jack Kerouac School of Naropa University. During my time there, I recognized I was surrounded by a sea of talent – much of it undiscovered in the world at large. In order to create a platform to exhibit such talent, and create a community to support it, I decided to develop a publishing company and a literary arts journal – *Monkey Puzzle*. I've been fortunate to receive and publish work that continually pushes the boundary of contemporary American literature, of which Adam Perry is an essential part of.

As publisher and editor of *Fotographs of Bones*, it was easy to ride the wave of Adam's experience and rhythm. Much of modern American poetry strikes me as so abstract that not only is the meaning lost, but it's hidden. This is not the case with *Fotographs of Bones*. Here is a poet who exposes himself, naked and raw, crying and rejoicing with the music of the spheres in its true and metaphorical sense. His book left me with a "mind full of song," which makes sense as Adam is not only a poet, but an accomplished musician as well. "With my conscience and my original heart," here's to "my harmony on my hereafter," and here's to yours.

Nate Jordon
April 3, 2009
Boulder, Colorado

Introduction

The honor of reading this manuscript at 5am fireside was like sneak-previewing a live performance before the curtain rises, revealing the technical magic of stage and the emergent depictions that incarnate to inhabit that space. The gears turn as meaning arrives and at once is encountered. Meeting the adroitly written *Fotographs of Bones* - a collection of numerous hybrid processes, eloquent notes on the impressions left from oscillating in life with ineffable, musical tides and the reflections and refractions like those of aurorae - can bring one to a trailhead, freeway, a field, or dawn.

If you are thirsty for lush embodiments of fervent and refreshing candor where double-pointed realities give rise to crisp imagination without lacking sentiments of grit, leather comes to pulse again: Adam Perry illuminates the rawness of exposed sensation[s/ex]periences through inspired filters. Fusing memory with moment-to-moment messages creates portals where reading transcends foraging through words for signs of life. Adam's words, like water - water that is translucence - will look you in the eye of this profound and bold composition. This poetry seems to have necessitated itself to the pages, humbly forging itself out-of-pocket for perspective built from dancing light and shadow that once was lost in mistuned voices. Catching up with time, each line reads whole, it seems, in a modern-era, where prophetical whim and relationship occurs actively.

It wasn't until landing at the last page of this manuscript that I even noticed the fire needed tending or my numb toes, which is to say that I was then acutely aware of having been worm-holed, cajoled, lullabied, and impulsively projected through "the curve within an echo," layers of cosmic journey residue, of critical tenderness, and the lazy desire to be entertained yet not possessed by this artful writing. Suddenly, the world of creative expressions opened upon the spun planes and membranes of what textured and permeable nucleus Adam concocted with his pen in his throat, laptop in the secure cage of his ribs, and printer between his lanky legs, coaxing his ego to brim with honesty while purging the facts in a sometimes fanciful and largely shameless display of bridging reality and descriptive chasms.

We infrequently find such dream (and simultaneously life)-like examples of creative force as this. In a frenzy of perfect timing, perhaps karmic vibration, you have in your hands a book of importance and living language. In this work, the mode, the voice, form, tone all dissolve into pure qualia as the amorphous music in these pages lends mental caresses and moot emotive responses that, regardless of consequence, are ready with "fire and faith" to stimulate "where below love is liquid," flowing, and available, and where the spaces between hold muses for the breath of the intellect. Here you will meet the writer soul-borne without buffers or margins, aside from those in type.

Fotographs of Bones: Three Seasons of Poetry is a testament to work that is honest and alive; through the poignant surface and simple depth of this writing by Adam Perry (his first solo collection of poetry since 2000), you will be invited to hear an aperture opening, or in his words, how "a glacier drops into a princess womb."

Irene Joyce
March 16, 2009
Boulder, Colorado

Sudden Death // Simple Man

When the sun went down on White Sands, the Lord's Prayer bled the rational from the moment I emptied my shoes until I found twisted sleep in the back of a truck, smuggling silence into Santa Fe. I couldn't speak when I died and,

not able to hear my sins, St. Peter led me into love for a while until the mistake was realized; I stammered the Tao of Ordinary Life and confessed my way home, back into an empty chair in Count Basie's Orchestra.

My parents had to order for me at restaurants until I left for college & in the 7th grade I once stayed on the phone for an hour without speaking to a girl who liked me. We listened to each other's breathing and the sound of two different TV shows

exchanging dialogue. When I was born, my eyes were wet with morphine; when my mother passed out, jazz trumpet shot through my somber mouth where a cry should've been. I had graduated from the rhythm section but wasn't old enough to

mime the stentorian warnings. Billie Holiday took over. Between washing dishes and writing adult books, I was annoyed by the wanton voice of God: "please" and "yes!" and then "here is your sex without love," but I held my breath and my cure until my troubles drank viscous adhesive and spat off a pier in San Francisco to bond a pair of shared genitals. Although your tears end up in my stomach,

my American conscience says "as a man, I'm not supposed to write like a woman; as a woman, I'm not supposed to hold both your hands while I swallow you or look down in all honesty, meeting your open eyes when we both ejaculate something

wholesome & metallic." I stopped in the middle of a winter hike to read you a story, but you were in another poem and had to look away. We hadn't made love in two days and I felt a woman growing inside me where a child used to push his way through my larynx with two little fists, wondering how I felt about talking or whether any of this is real. Just then, the phonograph slipped on icy steps and the needle skipped over any record of my life before jumping in the Pacific and suffocating

the courage to swing without shock. If this is the center, it's like a devil on the moon, waving back on a clear day; it's the rhyming between beloved and betrothed, breaking a brown egg on my face so you can't see my lips moving and it's just a mood. When you come home, my grey flannel suit won't have a paycheck in its pocket or an erection underneath, just the smell of whiskey stolen from the back of your throat when we shower together fully clothed. The uniform of the day

is a perfect body and an emotional smile, gracious and hopeful, staggering home before you have a chance to lie or change into your blue skin, which is not your sweat I taste, your essence I say "hello" to, or the spirit we share, but at least it's you.

My umbilical moon gave birth to an automobile to escape my poetry - she said she'd have a purpose in life if I called her once a week - and I'm growing a tiger lily from each of my shoulder blades to embrace your feminine mystique, which is neither you or me but a confluence between shattered cells and the dawn of healing I remember from before we were born. It was like dying without wings, expecting the angels to shrug: "one of us is rotating; one of us is naked, barely holding on under the weight of water, and the hard sound of a recorded piano says one of us is sliding and breathing heavy until the next life,

wondering what the other one wished for." I can see our sudden skin in the dark and hear simple songs in the knots of your lower back; as you bend into me, many small notes are transposed like sheet music covered in cum each time we split and sing, rolling r's while touching tongues as if there's a world I'm inventing between lemon and sponge,

broken and divine. The irony is a smooth chest and the imperfections of blue paint on an Asian face - a smattering of sun you move through with elegance, not knowing I see or seeing that I know…your explosion wears pajamas and swims in old orange juice, putting out a cigarette on my exposed heart

as if it would keep me from death. Your hands are wet, covered in the kind of "us" that we can spread around when we expand and spin, and the song is where I sleep while writing this for people laying cement in my stomach, running until wide open and then losing sight of what's beautiful

when you are all too beautiful. Hi. I need to tell you "hello, there's a pain in my head. There's someone worrying about me - are you sure my feet don't smell when I come home?"

Or am I too old for my age? "I was born at a very young age."

Walled together, each time we're out of shape // in of touch, you slow down and the Earth gets fasterfaster; children are watching with crossed arms [serious] and what could be more serious than a lolli- pop? Tell me. Don't cover your eyes unless it's with my mouth. Perhaps the children resent our colorless positions as mediators of immunity.

My tongue was wearing a seersucker coat (cotton or rayon, usually striped and literally milk and sugar) when I ran it along the curves of an acoustic guitar, extremely loud. When I was 19 I bought LSD from a stranger, drove a few miles into Hershey, PA (the Land of Chocolate) and fucked an old friend in the shower of a dirty motel room, against the moldy wall from which she got an infection. She turned her head once, looked back at me with eyes like glazed donuts and obviously wanted to watch the expression on my face or hear me say something. I didn't want her to kiss me or see me with my shirt off, but I came outside her and she said rainbows were shooting out of my cock. I said that I was a golden teenager hearing Neal Cassady's proud tune with copper brains

and I never said a word. Look at the snow. You didn't hear any of this.

One Month Apart

I.
The end of time is a natural gesture:

when I last created a world,
tears fell all over my pleasure -
she held me like a life-force, too tight
                    and broke my castle walls

Generosity spoke about straight lines,
the release of silver expectations,
male scriptures

                                        insulting
            because I don't want to fall asleep;

I want to menstruate with you
and conduct an orchestra of reception,
something unconscious for a shared conscience:
            sight-read   and   out-ride

"This energy doesn't control us."

One of my past lives was a mannequin,
not passive but inebriated,
and the opposite of your grace
                        exploding forever

"The illusion was changed"

        I burned a batch of phenomena,
        slipping sex into the unknown,
        moaning for neither pleasure nor procreation
                but the blind-sided beauty out of body:
                mutual ascension
                we can't hold

II.
Anytime I fall asleep under someone shining,
the birth is apparent in a blue collapse

Nourishing is a theft:
I slouch and curl in response to a sigh
or give you everything
                              interwoven
as if my hands and feet felt a certain way
rather than understanding everything about you
I can't touch with my skin

        My senses are in you:

                the top of a tall sun that meets a tree-line
                like an ability to grasp that we change each moment
                with socks kept on during a transcendent exchange
                of freedom and fluid
                as a glacier drops into a princess womb

III.
There was a knot in my soil through the summer heat

                Some dark body stood on stretched toes
                to meet my only pure memory with a single lie
                and the end result was mercury on my tongue,
                gullibility and confusion down a dry throat
                subtly unbuttoned on a wave
                whose black salt tastes like home

                I felt a lot of confirmation in a ceremonial swim
                although you pushed me in

Fire and Faith

The way music enters my veins
and leaves my fingers cold,
unable to write or touch the walls
where photographs of stillness hang
like heartbeats pounding,
vibrates the warm stone
always seen by strangers.

Look at my hands,
the found flesh where soft moments swallow
every painful second,
every forceful silence,
as you swallow my skin
and wait for my face to become human.

This healing rhythm turns over in the dark
like the young hands of the dying,
steadily making incisions
where the patient mind is prone to tremble,
sliding down a silky throat
as pinwheels explode inside a chimney.

Laugh at your mind in the snow
where desire waits for life
and bodies (trained to end this submission)
signal separation
by decisively inhabiting each other –
cascading downward, upward, sideways,
independent

stealing sequence while time is asleep.

Against the ones who wait,
my bed is language that caresses;
my holy dreams are comfort that envelops
and exhales brilliant light,

although one day it's triumphant summer
and the next we travel entwined in a coma.

In defiance, I am vibrant;
I smile at blank faces like immortality
and raise a cold, inspired hand
to nourish an overflow of honesty and heat.

The sound of our street is a siren, a whole home,
not a sheep in a broken shed, falling out of life
toward gentle rest.

All I can give you are the vowels in my name,
a corduroy soul who may whisper (no expectant sigh)
and help crush the concrete
where
below
love is liquid.

God Don't Humor Me

Think about the event of birth
your birth
how you entered writing
and imagined being here
the way you stitch the body with the sky
or another concept

My time is only a character:

"the space of partnership
does not begin with two bodies
but two versions of a body"

God has become absorbed
in my simple process,
a desire displayed
in another kind of work

I have a feeling: hunger

We never talk about the future
except the body narrative

We stay in to make love
except it's made us whole,
the dyslexic movement of our hands,
our emptiness filled with come

We've been here an hour
and I forgot to begin trying;
I forget to stop sharing
          everything I have
          everything I am

God doesn't need me –
the breakdown is glamorous

God is the kind of person
who can do anything he wants
have anyone or anything he wants
& experience anything he dreams

God will smile and rise
to greet a friend
but his expression does not change
when I enter a room –
the heat is too early
for honors
like new feelings

God don't humor me –
I need to get out of the sun
and move through sleep
as a sentence grows

God has everything
and has to do nothing
but respond to narration, sexual advances,
gradual burning of nerves
and rhapsody

Us and them:
a kind of girl and a kind of dog

God is a sign of loyalty
and also bondage;
God's offspring are elusive and disturbed –
they make you happy

God is a starting point,
an event between time and poetry
before you're on the page
flipping freedom // frustration

God is in denial of anything un-whole
of everyone who is lost in love,

feeding the text,
the fissures you return to
like language or the knowledge
that you have nowhere to stay

God has equal passions
very important
like the sound of a stranger's shoes
toward you
down a corridor
I don't know

but her intellect makes me feel
like a child

Dear Horizon,

It could have been an anchor I pushed into you, but the pull was something like a lighthouse. Perhaps we're a wildfire "because of what happens between ellipses and the continuation that we make love so well we recover our virginity." I see the city, but we can exist here all-knowing and unconscious, because we're moving. We mystery: man and wom(b)an(d) vice and never versus - a reversal. Who has the authority to push and pull heaven and hearth from both sides of variability? If only it was like a book with cylindrical binding in the center - pages inside and out, an author given peace to please - light room on a dark horse - a shape in shadows exists while you enter and by no means exit; an image speaks with no prevention, only echo fire. Jump off a building holding hands - what's the chance you'll fall on someone you love like an eclipse? Would you recognize sex from a print of my fantasy palm? (my son's line; my head line; my archer and flame and mineral line) Perception is the story of destiny; how we're always right on time, stumble and discover we're home, wiping stroboscopic genitals with sun-dried rags to prepare for free will. So breathe into my character, give me an overabundance of names to balance all those unnecessary superlatives on the exclamation points of a first kiss that happens every day. Circles are the only Lord of Light; they draw all possible combinations back and forth together and feather in orbit. A universal magnetism, desires tamed through indulgence vis-à-vis how blood bleeds: causal, astral, fizzle, stop and repeat. In essence, I would use your face...a photo of your grace...to describe what and how I'm feeling, but some people are out of love, so out of wearing skin that up is down and nothing moves anyway. We have become a most-favored instrument, a means of expression. Do this harmony on my hereafter, because the common gender is obsolete:

Love,
Adam

Bad Thoughts Escape Through Holes in the Page

The origins of my Gods are not so definite.
And thus, you'd be homeless
if I lost my poems.
You'd call me from a payphone in Los Angeles,
inquiring about alchemy
but I'd be empty of new material
and struggling to recall past lives in verse,
having burned the old.

But
you'll be safe in death
like beauty in the second world
where I wait for you.
Your life will be projected on brick walls at night,
in the comfort of summertime,
your earthly journey coaxed to kiss me
and communicate in celluloid,
kissing my mind in thin air,
dreaming so far above sea-level as to cry wind.

But don't go to sleep:
elect an affinity,
masturbate an oxy-moron,
levitate your self into exquisite meditative verse
in the sky,
where I am sheltered.

An Allegheny of Divine Wisdom

There must be somewhere in America I can call home,
because lately my grandfather sends love
from the bottom of the Ohio River
and traces invisible steps up and down South Side slopes
where our ghosts dream of endless bridges over dirty water
and forget entire seasons
like generations isolated in a steel town
they can't leave.

He still lives there underwater,
with my conscience and my original heart;
he scratches cracking green paint from his forehead
when I try to write;
he knows I lay naked and young with a girl one night
on the banks of the Monongahela, kissing
and pissing gold into the summer water,
drinking the city back in like iron
that used to grow there by the river
and harden in the center of my raw stomach
as if the shape of the city would tell my insides the flavor and intent
of an unwashed mind.

You could play the harmonica on Carson Street
until my eyes and ears were gone;
you could sail from the birth of my city to the depths of New Orleans,
unable to focus or forget
failures and faults at the fork of three rivers,
and I'd still make it mine.

Pantoum for Irene Joyce
February 19th, 2008

Put your faith inside me
if my voice is not enough
when you refuse to be pretty
and touch me where he can't see

If my voice is not enough
when you train yourself to hurt
and touch me where he can't see,
you're using the wrong words

When you train yourself to hurt,
someone will always be mesmerized;
you're using the wrong words
if you have so much faith

Someone will always be mesmerized
when you refuse to be pretty;
if you have so much faith
put your faith inside me

Body

My muse // I swear
you were humming.
I heard you whisper
"I am a child."

Since I can remember,
the dream door has been locked;
so many lines in cum-creation rhyme;
unwilling concubines leave me nothing
but a place to sleep – one more rest
and then swim in a poison ocean

love you the best.

When you forget to breathe,
don't call on me.
Make a lover out of clay

she glows without me.

You recommend me to the divine
but I am minutes late to be dipped in gold.
Words aren't enough,
so you remain a satellite behind me.

These bones are weak.
Brain damage balances friendship with the future,
separates the last moment of creation-cum
from the truth below what sad reflection
soaks good and long the souls of our present
in the notion of eyesight
neither stable nor blurred

this street's colored the parts I love.

This light gives birth to a stranger
poking through my skin.

this story is over

Ballad

I'm pretending to sleep
all the space I need
in a valentine like aqua (*tanta piacere*)
floating fresh as if Tom Waits was on the phone
saying you've let your hair down.
Watch me roll it soft across eighty-eight keys
with all your fingers in the right place,
the only phrase
rising.

But the real thought was that it's strange
you're not next to me in the heat
and the pleasure of kissing time,
missing jazz at blackest a.m.
Strange you're somewhere else
awake and dreaming, pushing a wheel
with tired bones // white chocolate
when in some split little time we could be waiting.

Living in light is hard to forgive –
I know you'll forget my plate full of cherries
& remember the transcription of many cascading notes
after socks come off.
Wandering home,
I'll take my time;
I'll remember death.
I'll paint you from memory
on the banks of three rivers.
My mother will ask why I don't have the sun
but I'll think of your hands
and the instinct of burning Denver:
somehow the cavern is mine with no silver horn,
not even sharp drums but almost 3 a.m.,
sweat given back through a candy straw.

The future keeps me cool

like chains across my chest
and words leave a mark you can read in the mirror:
luscious, late for dinner, western believers
are you and I.

The means to the coast I remember
(S.F. to L.A. and Monterey beside)
are the same as driving naked,
sitting up with a stone in mind
or speaking naked (that small-talk
we're missing)
down Highway 1 to beautiful techno uplifting
with a busted heart:
telling everyone "I love you"
but only coming for me.

Although,
who comes around these days
but treasury skeletons, exit-seekers sipping marrow
while you write on my eyelids from across town
and I write your id like a gospel shout?
All that's clear is crossed arms
and the signal on your blushing truth of a face:
just a saxophone (or gentle other end-time entry
like Donald Byrd)
centered on sex like quicksand.
Maybe no decision to kill the canary
but watch for my light as you slip in at all hours,
all visions without voice but lies locked –
you don't even test the water, but I live down here.
I grew up in that moment when we met beneath a cloud
but only learned to sing as it passed by.

The only decision I make is to stay honest,
keep your heart beating in the switch and glow,
not a drop lost but a cost reimbursed,
wet as you walk, blind as you talk
(*piano   forte*   angelic)

but beg me to stop when you're raw like a poem
stapled to a telephone pole and poisoned with love
in our pistol eyes.
What a challenge just saying "goodnight."

So no more smoke and drink, just skin stuck together,
((what's familiar so new))
alone together,
tiny bites and a busy street through my head
to tell us why it's day or night.
You've got wheels and wrong-doing to move me,
but let's stay right here:
Dexter Gordon is 'round the line (call waiting)
and here I go back to pretending...

Grace

[[[[[[[[[[[[forgive me if I'm too-bold]]]]]]]]]]]]]]]
but I felt/feel

[H]ealed.
Your grace sent me to some pure limbo
and I'm still there.
Your skirt rose and fell
like a cloud I slept thru, contorted ————————————————————
this must be you: the music of motion,
all of heaven down here
       in
       the
       middle
where   we   move.

[E]ntering songs of rain
and hands of one mind,
which is a means to plug each other in;
wetness from sweat to a singing sun that pours;
born to be (not) either/or and (not)for-long fiction
like strands of one skin,
sparks held and (dearly) hurled mouth-to-mouth,

[L]ocked:
    (?) -->
    (!) -->
    (?!) -->
    (?) --------------->
    (!!!.....)

[L]earning a consecrated language, wondering
what runs down legs in twilight
but future-fluid and phantom fingers
flashing/laughing:
the reason I write oceans

[O]ver and over, not stereotypical intimacy
or her or us but *this*:
these two vessels of God
uncontrolled/unconscious and
(like the slowly-revealed, silly & surely-entwined girl
with giant sunflowers for stilts)
so easy to hold and so hard to let go
go go
                    (so we grow).

Dream Over Middle West in Seat 14C

Tell me if the sun that shines
thru man and woman, legs spread,
toes touching wide
is Abraxas or a soft reply,
clutching four walls in darkness
to find a light: the devil in heaven.

I heard another fantasy up there,
before sleep on an airplane
smiling crooked over middle west,
no stars no time no thing beneath
a bell-rung vision of entering my bed
after time (not fireworks) gone
to find you within and without confusion.

But the book I dreamt, sleeping alone
in hot Pennsylvania dawn
was of singing "I'm addicted to your aging face"
down an old hallway,
upsetting Tiffani Parrish
("stop your loud singing; it's 4 a.m.!")
before driest morning
and welcoming an altruistic, transparent figure
like a rising lion joining me
without illuminated features,
just a face and heart (openly) becoming ours
in clear physical darkness
equaling return-words.

Shirtless, hands circling then loving
heroine breasts, drops of life
around two halo-heads exchanged
with revolving lips conquering a lock,
everything wet in the black moon
of a pre-sentiment room.

We talked in the dark,
something about me carrying your bicycle home
as spoken words marked the middle of a new planet
and then faded as alone I sincerely woke
with zipper open,
engine exposed somehow in the center,
and felt you
new.

The Foretaste of a Soul Field

Around my wrist, someone uncommon

I remember opening my chest,
exposing rare bones, previously sanded-down
and liquid from a place of love long un-used

dust upon dust.

What   still works
might not be what I wanted
or,
as God said:

"in sequence"

We think of nourishing the un-born
rather than bathing in the *nowness*
of life inside a million photo-booth pictures
framed as one
            when instead, as she said:

"we are the outside world

my face is yours

lie down and roll into me, natural

allow us to listen"

The miracle is in bloom,
shifting in the sky accidental,
pillars to nothing all torn up

Don't forget:
my feet wonder how to sleep alone
with the horns of angels striking sunrise // saliva

as if the many small words from lack of rain
were for anyone else

Bring me flashes:
who I am, balanced, humming;
sticks around sun-designed shade
being mind
        full of song
All over dreams I came
an entire heart by psalm -
on the verge of waste, in the heat of blood
my mind pounding where an overanalyzed cock could not,
she turned to me and carved a life from who we are

We met space with acceptance & forgiveness,
demystifying un-condition with exchanged skeletons,
paper potion passing through each orifice
like the life of a lamb

Take A Moment and Listen

Listening makes you vulnerable -
an old friend growing up, smiling
'cross the hallucinogenic classroom of keyed-up
quiet-shrieking wonder
knowing silly is sacred in a universal mood -
she is careful without pitch.
She turns rose-red when speaking,
concerned white when watching others interact.
But you...
unless you steal my eyes so many people enjoy me conscious,
your way, slightly broken:
                    stop.

A combination of edible notes in the R.O.Y.G.B.I.V. scale
are an oral fixation in heaven
or just a longing to love your stomach with fingers in flux,
depending on how we're sitting,
open, natural or a novel
like bottomless rainwater eased into standing up hard,
not with anyone but who's in my pocket
transposing a short-story with Sinclavier,
flesh-breathing dragon un-tucking my shirt
to fresh potion felt-feather devotion
with an active mind:
don't think so much...
time is running out.

II.
A symphony of place:
She   is   all   over -
there is sound inside me that is us
and peripheral landscape like a thousand pores
at the end of our beginning,
which penetrates the quiet perimeter with small heartbeats like
police bells,
new-born near-loves being fed with spoons of rust connecting

dust in Jewish warnings
which decay to small-engine, cross-pollinated flights
splitting the sky way down through tongues that say hello
and a pleasant sneeze or two:
cosmic sweet-and-sour never lost, so erect in wet grass.
One hand follows hers while the other hides my shy sex
on the way to whatever bent-over music we create
without looking away.

Mountain Sun Poem

an "exquisite corpse" with Irene Joyce

his harlequin evening has pinstripes and Polos
convinced that a costume can buy you drinks

the glasses clink and the ice chills fingers
gripping social resistance,
then the sound drowns
and thinks itself into textures so respectable
no nakedness can compete

vibrations compete where days are emptied
our cymbals penetrate
but be kind to a room full of strangers –
give us the blues with your warm hands;
watch the sun roll down a silent street
subduing the snow

when you were white
I filled in the colored lines
with strange and strong //
I made your red face kind
and co-existent
as you touched your blushing cheeks
with memories and monsters,
closets full of now and then,

childhood fears all grown up

when you skinned me,
I felt cold for a moment
then lost fingernails
when my friends took me home

if you had four arms
you could point us in all directions
'til we forgot recovery is a mask

the sun would roll down our backs
like so many small songs
that were a piece of your piece;
so like a peach-pit,
a hard stone to crack,
put it to planting
put it underground
way down there
under the weight of city structures
that hold you in boxes toward the sky
down below the poorest punctuation:
the dollar sign that,
unlike a finger pointing to the moon,
won't or can't mean more
than what it appears to symbolize

Black Mariah

drip:
my grandfather was in the war
holding marijuana
psychotic break or both

like rain on a windshield
I can't take you
with me
or rubble changing phones
holograms
experience bodies lost and found
go home dizzy film

unable to stare through doors
in sync the road stops

I disappear,
charging out of the poem
the sound of my pencil
direction // time // concept
hold my head
your home

give me a seizure;
I like the dark
open bay windows
San Francisco ocean
harbor images
beyond high recovering bodies
put a baby together in nine months
other suicides

this many faces
revolving after each fire
resembles a police wagon
following sunlight

to remember
a fracturing

such as Casablanca,
scratchboard white,
a layering of colors

to remember
let go of the scene:
images come
and don't follow the dream

swallow a bottle of light
sanctuary will be lost
Alaska standard time
brings back memories
best seller of my life

weeks before death,
the chance of snow skipping stones
felt like static:
without ice, we survive on scatter
acoustic // electric
in that space

without our fragments,
I was falling
          fallen
      flattening
deep emotion

Folding Up

an "exquisite corpse" with Shane Clements

All the time glowing from two soil spots into an arch
(the carpet is short and black; there is no confetti)
all the light from a long morning
twists a heart recognition folded into giving
touching forehead and eyes and lips
to a sunrise that missed me

And even now, the dandelions are gossiping
& spreading their rumors –
the other half of who brought me here can tell about you
and empty my pockets like a fifth of steel

The blinds are pulled down;
light is creeping through the slits

It's morning
and I'm sure the door is warming up to me…
one more day
and I might believe

The Precipice Went Slack

At the beginning of a land-locked way home,
a sign read:
"ice
may
exist"

If given permission, water would become solid;
if asked a question,
my eyes would finish your sentences,
already blended like whiskey & coke aimed
on a precipice so tempting
as an orchid sexually attractive
enough that male wasps would love it
to the point of ejaculation

Boulder Camels

In early 2009, scientists in Boulder, CO discovered a box of tools buried at least 13,000 years ago. Protein residue on these tools proved that animals not normally associated with North America, such as camels and rhinos, used to live in what is now known as Colorado. Using a cut-up process akin to the Burroughs/Gysin method, I manipulated the contents of an article on this amazing find.

A giant said:
"the wooly wetter artifacts Bamforth discovered
would be an axe where scientists found the disturbed astonishing."

Sloths,
including Clovis-age Americans,
elegantly unresolved ice-age elephants
under small plates of Boulder's soul
and specifically impacted knives
because I've been somewhat ritualistic.

They discovered rhinos crafted on an ego
down to fell blades the result of a suspected small comet.

Prominent anti-sera cats named Robert
resemble saber-toothed genera shovels I've shipped tightly
into double-bitted caches
during a catastrophic test

The Front Rage believes other artifacts were the end years,
the result of prominent area species still whole –
13,000 utilitarian mammals crafted from the residue I desired
and extinct because I'm lacking the protein positive
to own horses.

Living in a Cliché: Boulder Creek, 7 p.m. June 25, 2008

Soon enough,
the creek we walked across will freeze
and I'll turn the record over –
but first, you have to come home.

I sit writing on rocks as the sun falls,
with something to give
if you want it.

The creek is music;
nature is here and gone;
insects make love, too –
but I still dream of the city:
pavement with songs growing out;
streets with demons up and down;
me drunk with friends who love me honest
graceful wandering,
getting to the bottom of truth
where the ocean meets a high-rise.

I belong in the town
but have seen my self here
in mountain
water
nowhere.

Fall Down Riding

Two hours on a sweet black cruiser
spinning legs and sweating brown angel flesh
indefinitely one half of ever-love,
I crawled up and down a dry path
in the long lust of getting lost in the state where I sing,
vision thick with prairie dogs and Boulder bath-water.

Climbing on air, I barely hung on to comfort
but succeeded in thumbing the mystic fret-board in my mind,
attaching wings to an improvisation-turned-melody
like petals giving flight to a mighty vehicle
                    waking up   together.

In a glance with eyes closed,
I saw the reason we're a wildfire, St. Theresa:
East and West words
gathering all the instruments
to play an entire heart by song:
"who ever came to life in a car crash,
was given birth in a train-wreck,
kissed in double-time with limbs over drums
after an introduction so patient and dramatic
the audience fell asleep
or took to fucking in the bathroom?"

I ride through nature, cracking Indian land,
pretending to hear colors like what's on bark and rain;
can't help but see mandolins coming down,
not sure what's a mirror // who's a prince.

So we're bound to science, swallowing spoons of chocolate
I will erect
like baby teeth full of distance in motion:
nobody
waiting
any
more.

Descending Poem

VI.
The obsessive human making music scribbles scripture.
So if writing travels between pages,
here is a threshing ground for your thinking:

religion is a competition –
I see her licking my fingers clean
and bombing a lack of discipline
with silver spiders,
chalk-dust conscious
where self was.

There is rain in the small city
but the language of all things –
at least those you choose not to remember –
watches a fire in the valley
below a Zen mountain
where Kerouac sleeps
drunk.

Thus, there is no identity but a plane
tail-spinning through the sun
while I drink Rooibus tea on the moon
and stare at a blank page.

V.
Human spiders drink religion
below silver mountains
where language sleeps.

Thus, in tail-spinning scriptures
the chalk-dust city is bombing you small
where Kerouac travels obsessive
and Zen fingers lick the ground drunk.

In the valley where my thinking is clean,
here is the conscious rain that scribbles music
on blank pages.

IV.
Music sleeps on spiders
where the city is obsessive
and language licks small scriptures

in chalk-dust conscious.
Kerouac is clean,
tail-spinning,
writing on mountains
 and the valley is drunk.

III.
The city is drunk;
music is the mountains;
and language sleeps on Kerouac.

II.
Kerouac sleeps
and the *music* is drunk.

I.
Kerouac is drunk.

Haiku

The top of my heart
makes a sound like falling leaves
when we say hello

The blacksmith
made a heart from a bomb
and washed his hands

Stumbling with eyes closed
the lights from morning thought
fell from my hand

Down winter stairs
you rang the Earth's alarm
by falling

Under a warm tongue
crocodile tears fade
like lines on a highway

The rain has not come
so the sound of the past
is all I hear

A gentle disaster
sat with crossed eyes
in a town he forgot

No one ever looks down
from an airplane headed home
and sees himself

I had never seen
a hummingbird without wings
until you couldn't speak

The taste of tender eyes
was simple in the divine
simple in your touch

Engraved on a stone
underneath a fragile head
was the memory of a girl

The selfish writer
closed his eyes
and pretended to talk

When I remembered
the summer mouse
I remembered sleeping alone

The curve within an echo
looked back at me
when it became wet

The modest sister
sabotaged her re-memory
by never knowing

Distance between downtown
was the cloud of smoke
where I was born

The cafe waitress
with a sad and lined young face
has many regrets

White on a sidewalk
won't become ice
because I don't drink anymore

Sitting is something
to prevent rust on the face
inside my old mind

The song in these strings
washed away before I had a chance
to grow old

Two little guitars
had a wooden child
and spent their days alone

The end of a fire
in our stone cottage
is the image of home

Somefarwhere You Shined

*In March 2009, I was hypnotized by Murray Klickstein, a 79-year old former Boston
professor and psychologist who had not performed a hypnotism in almost twenty years.
Part of this poem came to me while in the altered state Murray helped me reach.*

I.
Alive,
my body was shaking // floating,
my feet twitching extraordinarily (I was told later)
and my breath shook like a great swaying oak
in a thunderstorm:
I had so much to say in silence
independent of glowing flesh.

In shivering movement
incredible crown to incredible toe,
my stomach twirled, flowing like newborn butterflies
aimed to carry my insides to revelation.

I barely kept my self from intensely laughing,
not at the silly spectacle of my suspended mind
but because I was so happy.

If he never brought me back - so what?
All I knew was nothing,
no dreams, no expectations,
only angels in the golden flakes of dissolving soul
we call "me."

"I can speak if I want to,"
me said.

"Make friends with your stuttering,"
he said. "It's part of what made you
you."

I smiled and breathed deep;

I yawned over and again,
inhaling relaxation.

3,
2,
1:
when I opened,
looked at my vibrating hands,
felt my joyfully-trembling organs
and saw the light around my quivering toes
no different from my pulsating hair and shivering life,
I tried to speak and my mouth barely separated, barely moved,
like walking thru bitter cold and finding warmth where words and lips
and faith are frozen.

"My spirit is shaking," I thought.
"Thank you," I said.

II.
The experience of hypnotism
is falling asleep to blossom,
letting go to find something // someone new
in your old world to embrace.

Eternal life can only be this:
music is a form of amnesia,
although love is enough –
the crackling fire is all I heard in the dark of Zen
"so incredible" in the void love never needs to fill.

Farewell to the un-natural world of any burden
not erased with a dry morning kiss on partnered skin
that becomes wet with memory.

Returning,
I realized the healthy Yiddish voice sent me roving
around the universe un-alone and forgot to forget
clarity was clamoring for light

but there was nothing
and what is more beautiful?

He stood in front of the fire as I came back
and there was no divide -
young // old // awake // alive
happy // haunted // holy

Somefarwhere you shined too.

III.
Mother nature
earth collector
asked "what did it mean to you?"

I felt.

I fell in love with vibration // science // language
eating time and age again,
growing presumably outward
by pulling electric thread,
the door behind me
open.

My speech was welcomed in,
our truth saved by an incredible old-young man
caring // understanding // affecting // embracing,
closing peace on a watery brain.

An oblong box, an Orgone token accumulating
eighty years of learning what it means to relax
in a far-off place inside
us.

I don't know whether my speech was launched
from a cathedral-shaped hell that made me smile
and let go // hold on with my heart
but my hometown rolled its eyes

and (in a sad storm)
mourned the loss of a smoke-covered verse
with dark hair rolling blind with limited lines
spread wide in a notebook over Irish whiskey –
a portrait of James Joyce being psycho-examined
while dreaming of the World Series, three-pointers
and the 1950's.

"A finely-honed athlete is as beautiful
as a finely-honed mind,"
he told me.

And right about then,
my parents were watching television
while I levitated,
reading the inside of my dry skull
like sulfur-colored stone
no more superior to idols of America
than stuff that was once rotting
and now watches New Mexico suns set
like exploding smallness in rotation.

Everything was rock // everything is heaven
and that's enough. I will not
be compressed or go to school for memory.
I will not write 1,000 times
"the future seems late."

Comic books and World War journals
look at the Tao Te Ching like a cultural event
as if a young man without Sonic Youth and Converse All-Stars
becomes relevant in the spit of a wheel.

Spirit, let me sit naked with your poem
like an acoustic experiment,
a new direction in sincerity // sarcasm
and praise.
Don't drink too much.

IV.
Sensational mother, daughter, Zaydee
and co-muse drive through Sandoval County talking
with an old tape of Ginsberg reading "Mexico City Blues,"
bop haiku bleeding down the side of a Subaru
onto sunburned Indian land
thinking of a poem about how we hiked
"and looked for fucking rocks."

Kerouac locked himself in a bathroom-stall south of U.S.
chorus // cerveza // dope // bennies
ridiculous Catholic deconstructing pictures,
putting fire under Bird's honest visuals –
what Southwestern scenery-story smoothed
little blue star-stems in your tea.

In other words,
I want to camp // sing // sleep // and make love
in the White Sand we slid down,
the spine we sailed.
I don't get angry
but in my muscles the worry hurts,
the subtle changes are heavyweight
like a starting-line that keeps moving,
a synaptic wrap-around.

That kind of sand doesn't bury me –
the repetition of a lizard makes my consciousness a sieve
like the belly of a belly,
elegant chains over madness
which happily sunk into a shaft of light
when you asked would I close my eyes.

Moving around North America,
I want to give birth in the Red Sea
but the spray-painted Warhol skyscrapers of home-plate
(where Black Elk Speaks)
scarcely reach the other world
when I'm dyslexic without a moment

in of my mind.

I was reduced to the size of a Hopi playground,
writing my way out of desire // disaster
I could do more with
than talk.

You're easy to be with, Murray;
you capitalize on pauses as if my shaky thoughts
could morph into a ghost, alive
and italicized, walking eternal.

We aren't sure of the sequence –
the integration or invocation
(no religion is more than imagination
and "religion is the cause of
most of the world's problems") –
but I know about her.

I know about her
and I will always love.

Zen Poem
for Gerry Wick

Part 1. (Before *Sesshin*)

Faith is nothing new,
only in the round I hear everything:
sitting still,
sweat upon sweat,
learning there is no drug powerful as love;
no love powerful as nothingness;
and nothing like:

Zen is bones on the outside
bones outside are Zen
outside is Zen in my bones

Although, nothing is mine:
Narahari's face is this face is my face is your face
is our face is the face of
God is still not music, but at least we've begun

If I could forget myself,
I could remember the world,
such as:

Church St., San Francisco;
a spiritual materialist in Zen robes
visits the smiling corpse of Philip Whalen
in a chair, fat old Buddha loving New York Zen
like a fur coat to die in

Or Gas Works Park, Seattle;
a young man, shy
finds Coltrane blowing sheets of Zen on a passing cloud;
realizes nothingness even more but cannot share;
is a warrior in friendship and forgiveness and selflessness
but cannot answer the phone

Close your eyes:
the moment a child opens his
he is true nature, everything –
he is almost music.

Part 2. (During *Sesshin*)

I.
When I saw my shadow, there was nothing
and when I finally slept
dreams were replaced by you

My intention is to focus,
but in my nothing-mind
I want to tell everyone
you are here with me

I want to tell you:
no bell rings;
no mouth waters;
no skin is too dry;
no knees throb
and no dust reaches out for my heart

But I cannot speak
except to imagine
we'll never return from this moment

I am here to learn, to witness, to be

And although I've seen my shadow,
I am not given away;
I will never choose a path
but keep walking in four directions
until I learn about death

In silence, we know
our senses live and breathe.

We listen to our thoughts and send them away
because they are not us

We are one mind,
but I still want to love;
there is someone who may not love me,
who may never swoon if I cannot speak
but I still want to love

One mind wants her
to hear my thoughts now
except to imagine I'll never return
from this moment

II.
The universe sits on a shelf
in service,
listening, living
to put us together
not knowing we fear the end

Sitting cross-legged
in a dream around the earth,
I would rather know time with you
than be here in silence, with nothing
to look at but all the souls
I saw in a white wall
like shapes in the sky,
clouds walking independent
of arms and legs

III.
We went further inside
until I was gone

And all the while,
whenever I felt truly lost
there was music from a stranger:
"don't close your eyes;

If there are footsteps,
you're wasting time;
if you see me give up,
walk across the *Zendo* and
touch my aching back,
my cluttered monkey-mind,
with the hands of a child,
you've had visions too;
if there are ears listening to the wind,
you are wasting time -
stay here"

Three days of required silence and
four two-hour sessions of meditation a day,
high on being alive and alone,
made me turn over in a bed of no-self
and wonder whether to tell you
the shrinking space between us
feels like home

I felt cold air for a moment,
zipped up, walked along a river at 5 a.m.
and imagined my brain floating in saltwater,
though it was just the unfamiliar sensation
of being awake

You may have remembered a traumatic event,
knelt along the light between mountains,
and imagined a window opening,
birds bowing in like Buddha in tears,
but it was just the new feeling
of being on my mind

I took my shoes off in your dream,
read your letter in the dark,
and wondered if I set my sights too high,
too big, instead of seeking
what's beneath me,
or simply what's upstairs,

inside the waiting man

He can only turn around
and face his lack of self
in a quiet room with many others
sitting, realizing one mind,
making music by vowing silence

Asked about insights,
the waiting man thought clarity was an insight

He had no questions; he only wondered
why I need a muse,
because it was hard not to see your face
when there was nowhere to look but down –
perhaps I missed the point,
but I'm not sure I want that feeling
of nothingness all the time
because I would rather touch you

IV.
There is something left to be said
about discipline, customs
and grown men prostrating themselves,
giving themselves to the earth below,
to the invisible chaos of unreality
without a fight

And when I finally succeeded
in turning off that flow of thought
which is a great waterfall
where a gentle stream should be,
I was looking forward
instead of sinking down,
digging in to fall away

When there was no sound,
my mind stretched out
like the wings of an arrogant dragon

I counted my breath
until there were no numbers to remember
but I, you, we, me, they
and then nothing

Nothing caressed;
nothing spoke;
nothing soothed an aching stomach;
nothing walked alone with rare birds
after dawn; nothing skipped *"Dharma* Talk"
to write poetry
and no one knew I was gone
(except an old man who smiled)
because they were also found

We were all together without effort
but I still wanted to love
and music never went away
unless my thoughts were a song
and my self was a song
in that we are all one note
but I still love;
and when self is gone
I see you

V.
I remember Roshi sang to me
in simplicity: "do not waste time!"

He sings without speaking, knowing
"Dharma Talk" is forever but
service is for those who serve,
who pick and choose
joy and freedom. Don't tell me
what I'm here for:
Roshi says I'm here to follow my breath
because there are no adjectives in Buddhism

If there is nothing, then
there is nothing you can express

If there is no self,
there are no feelings

If there is nothing to be liberated from,
there is no freedom

If there is nothing to hurt,
there is no joy

If there is no single mind
there is nothing to know

but I know I wondered if you thought of me
because I'm still human
and if I shake the fence of no-thought
will you swoon?

All is well until I share my thoughts.

Worship, Salvation & Prayer

or

Sacrifice
Two Mediums Are Exposed
The Reader's Life Is Subject to Assault;
My Cock Was Exposed By Your Academic Text
Or High-Brow Sex

and

Sins Cope
Hands Broke
Bite the Sleep
You Suck
You Sin-Cope-Ate Rapture
And Rake The Leaves
In My Dead Grandfather's Backyard
As a Natural Topic
Only To Serve 'em To Me
As You Served My Ashes
In a Salad You Spoke Of
With Living Language

and

Sins Cope
Hands Broke
Bite the Sleep
You Suck
You Sin-Cope-Ate Rapture
And Rake The Leaves

In My Dead Grandfather's Backyard
As a Natural Topic
Only To Serve 'em To Me
As You Served My Ashes
In a Salad You Spoke Of
With Living Language

and

We Live Together
In a Transparent Sentence
Pain Was Raped
The Sign Was Shaped
Like Wet Paint
To Highlight An Act of Love
As a Feather Had To Be White

but

If You Learn My Blinking Speech
I'll Take The Eye Out
Of The Static Channel
Of The Fuzz Between Stations
Of The First-Person Sound I Swallow

also

To My Own Ends
There Was a Slip
For Him // For An Autobiography // For High-Low
That Says Something About Excess
Only Sitting Still While I Am Photographed
With a Face That Looks Like a Fever

Lodged Between Your Open Mouth
And a
Sub
Urban
Relation to Experimenting With New Bodies
Telescopes
Which I'll Never Need
To Make You New
Your Bold Feeling, Which Is Open
When I Arrive Good // Deep // 'Breathe'

although

You Ask Me To Think Of Daily Life As a Choir
And Your Falling Head Lands On My Work
Like a Sunrise with Clean Sheets

point out the stars
the atlas
& the chest

she is the hearer of all bones

Adam Perry was born and raised in Pittsburgh, PA and lived a double life as preschool teacher and rock drummer in San Francisco from 2002-2008. Adam studies writing and literature at the Jack Kerouac School of Disembodied Poetics and writes about music for *Westword* and *Boulder Weekly*.